In his new book the author of "Lost Paradise," of "Primer for America," "Strange Holiness," and "Collected Poems" brings out a group of poems which have grown from the experiences of his aviator son, a fighter pilot in the United States Navy. He includes also the marriage poem he composed for his daughter's wedding, and one or two poems concerned with the war.

But this new volume is more than a record of particular sons and daughters and wars. In it, as always, the poet goes on with his sharp etchings of the sad and beautiful country scenes, for which he has become famous throughout the nation. And he continues also with the record of his experiences of that strange and lovely light which changes the texture of common living into a mystic pattern running through all created being.

POEMS FOR A SON WITH WINGS

BOOKS BY ROBERT P. TRISTRAM COFFIN

POEMS
- CHRISTCHURCH
- DEW AND BRONZE
- GOLDEN FALCON
- THE YOKE OF THUNDER
- BALLADS OF SQUARE-TOED AMERICANS
- STRANGE HOLINESS
- SALTWATER FARM
- MAINE BALLADS
- COLLECTED POEMS
- THERE WILL BE BREAD AND LOVE
- PRIMER FOR AMERICA
- POEMS FOR A SON WITH WINGS

ESSAYS
- BOOK OF CROWNS AND COTTAGES
- AN ATTIC ROOM
- CHRISTMAS IN MAINE
- BOOK OF UNCLES
- MAINSTAYS OF MAINE

LECTURES
- NEW POETRY OF NEW ENGLAND
  (*Frost and Robinson*) (*The Turnbull Memorial Lectures,* The Johns Hopkins University)
- THE SUBSTANCE THAT IS POETRY
  (*The Patten Lectures,* Indiana University)

BIOGRAPHIES
- LAUD: STORM CENTER OF STUART ENGLAND
- THE DUKES OF BUCKINGHAM
- PORTRAIT OF AN AMERICAN
  (*The Author's Father*)
- CAPTAIN ABBY AND CAPTAIN JOHN
  (*Abby and John Pennell,* Brunswick, Maine)

AUTOBIOGRAPHY
- LOST PARADISE
  (*The Author's Life to His Twelfth Year*)

NOVELS
- RED SKY IN THE MORNING
- JOHN DAWN
- THOMAS-THOMAS-ANCIL-THOMAS

HISTORY
- KENNEBEC: CRADLE OF AMERICANS
  (*The Rivers of America Series*)

TEXT
- A BOOK OF SEVENTEENTH-CENTURY PROSE
  (*With A. M. Witherspoon*)

POEMS FOR
A SON WITH WINGS

BY ROBERT P. TRISTRAM COFFIN

THE MACMILLAN COMPANY · *NEW YORK*

1945

First Printing

A WARTIME BOOK

THIS COMPLETE EDITION IS PRODUCED
IN FULL COMPLIANCE WITH THE GOVERN-
MENT'S REGULATIONS FOR CONSERVING
PAPER AND OTHER ESSENTIAL MATERIALS.

PRINTED IN THE UNITED STATES OF AMERICA
BY THE VAIL-BALLOU PRESS, INC., BINGHAMTON, N. Y.

To

MY WINGED SON

ROBERT JUNIOR

ACKNOWLEDGMENT

Grateful acknowledgment is made to the following periodicals for permission to reprint poems which first appeared in their pages:

American Cookery, American Girl, American Mercury, Atlantic Monthly, Christian Science Monitor, Commonweal, Free World, Good Housekeeping, Ladies' Home Journal, National Parent-Teacher, New York Herald Tribune, New York Times, New Yorker, Pageant, Poetry Chap-Book, Saturday Evening Post, Saturday Review of Literature, Science Illustrated, Virginia Quarterly Review, and *Winged Word.*

CONTENTS

POEMS FOR A SON WITH WINGS

THIS DAY MY SON PUTS ON HIS WINGS

These wings with feathers strutted apart,
Place them now each side your heart,
Let them take you to the blue,
Through war, through death, to all things new.

You fly between two ancient hymns,
You have added the white limbs
To the yearning human four
Only the greatest old gods wore.

The dim dream of a soaring one
Is bone of your young bone, my son,
Hermes with his speed on him
And the burning Cherubim.

Use them well, these fierce wild things,
Make good use, my son, of wings,
Let no tons of silvery power
Keep your youth from gentle flower.

Wear your wings, young citizen,
Out of the flat world that has been
Into the new world which is round,
Which man can travel fast as sound.

The round world your wings will explore
Must have no closed heart, no closed door,
No black race, white race, yellow, or brown,
But only neighbors in one town.

No peaks, no valleys, no high or low
Your high and young blue eyes shall know.
Open your wings, son, and go fast
Over a brotherly world at last.

You who were so merry and fair
I have lost now to the air,
Little son grown tall! I speed
You on your high way to sow seed.

Make me, who your father were,
One with Abraham of Ur,
Who saw his seed as seed of light
Sown like stars across round night.

UPSTAIRS

My son who lives on thin air and high speed
Speaks poems that have shaped the shapeless air,
He takes up houses men cannot outgrow;
When he climbs clouds, he does it by a stair.
"I was upstairs that day," he says, that day
He went between high heads of Summer rain
And under meadows of lightning where the mists
Were turning into rice of icy grain.

My son returns from another universe
Where death is always watching like a hawk,
Yet speaks no hawk's high language, but a man's,
And old Greek gods are smiling in his talk.
The azure halls of winds are full of men;
Though wings may grow on each side of their head,
Their thighs are like the solid curves of hills,
Their lovely feet fit lovely earth they tread.

These new air-men go as children go
Calmly up old stairs to quiet and sleep,
As men go up to beds of love or death
On earth, foot after foot. They do not leap.
They go where all is windows, and a thing
That has no eyes through every window stares,
But they build out below them as they fly
The old strengths of men's childhood and safe stairs.

LOST SON

I do not know the turning
When the thing was done,
I do not know the hour
I lost my little son.

It was years ago, though,
And he was very small,
I loved him, but he no longer
Was with me there at all.

Some bright thing caught his fancy
And pointed him his way,
I did not know of his going,
He smiled so day by day.

He was there beside me,
And there's the sharpest pain—
It took so long to discover
He'd not be mine again.

O small son, now a tall one,
Whatever wars or woe
You go to, I'd give diamonds
If I could also go.

But since a father fathers
Tall strangers by his fire,
I bid godspeed and give you,
Lost son, my heart entire.

4

WIND FROM HOME

Along his plane an empty blue mile high
He heard the wind go sad and make a cry,
And in this alien heaven walled around him
He knew the wind of home had come and found him.
The wind away on his own azure coast,
That little south wind hanging like a ghost
On his room's eaves, even in fairest weather,
Had come a thousand miles. They were together.

It was the wind which has the sea inside it,
The men within his blood had learned to ride it
On cloth wings leaning white along the waves
Where some of them had found their blue deep graves.
Now he was riding it on his own kind
Of sails, with land and sea both left behind.
It was the old wind in this strange new weather,
Men in his blood and this man flew together.

He closed his eyes, and he was still a boy
Falling asleep with his bright newest toy
And hearing the wind that came in off the deep
Smoothing the waves that ran with him towards sleep;
And he was earlier boys with his blue eyes
Hearing the wind from sea that cries and cries:
In years that were and will be, now and forever,
Men and the sea and wings belong together.

HE KNEW WHO IT WAS

That day my winged son spun and fell
In fire and cold steel he knew well
Who it was who reached and drew
His parachute out white in the blue.

He could not think, he could not drop
Out of his deadly spinning top,
The dark came down over his eyes,
He came to, floating on the skies.

He opened his eyes held by the power
In a vast white opened flower
And rode with ribs curved over his breath
Above a meteor of hot death.

My son, who has never thought of the dim
Hereafter, with a smile on him,
Told me simply, right as rain,
His dead friend pulled him from the plane.

It was the friend he saw from the sky
Fall and in the white flames die.
They had lived high, brother and brother,
Each promised he would save the other.

His friend went first, he had to ride
And watch how his bright tall friend died.
And now when he faced into the black,
An arm came round him, drew him back.

A friend's arm is a thing that can
Reach very far to help a man,
It can come from behind far seed
Of nebulae when there is need.

MY HOME WAS FLOWERS OPENED

I leaned and looked at my old home below,
But it was morning-glories specked with snow,
Not islands, bays, and seagulls, not gray ledges,
But flowers opened with sun upon their edges.
Two thousand feet in under my winged seat,
My farm was glossy leaves veined sharp and neat,
Each elm tree had its shadow tied to it,
Squared fields made a geometry to fit
The airy minds of angels thinking light,
Great compasses had set wild nature right.
The only neighbors I saw besides the trees
Were six bright-banded cows the size of bees,
Stuck fast and deep in a slab of honeycomb,
And one short man bringing his long shadow home.
A huckleberry island on the flood
Burned with Autumn like a drop of blood,
The cedars came up towards me burning green,
Slender as seraphs with deep dark between,
Colored maple trees were coals of fire,
Long ledges were long threads of silver wire.
I saw deep into bays, they were designs
Of unbelievable and lovely vines,
The channels in the mud were tendrils growing
Out from dark water. Everywhere it was snowing
Under me, and it was minute gulls
Of friends' boats with the foam each side their hulls.
Nowhere did transparent colors stop.
That was not my island but a drop
Of amber lying lonely on the sea.
There was no wind below, but every tree
Leaned in equal loveliness due south,
Each island had a white bone in its mouth.
Nothing moved below me, boats stood still
As they cut the ocean. This was the sill

To the door of heaven. What I had thought
Was coast with islands out beyond was not
Common land and water but sunshot places
Where men should all have flowers for their faces.

FOR THE YEAR-OLD SON OF A WAR-FLYER

Astyanax cried at the spread
Plumes on his brave father's head,
You have no fear of such high things,
Your father's head is two tall wings.

You are a very modern son,
You expect your father to run
On the white clouds of the sky,
Fathers are beings made to fly.

Fathers are winged things, they come home
From the perilous white foam
Of thunderheads, from war's alarms,
And take you up in cool strong arms.

You expect your father to go
Higher than eagles, high as snow,
And yet be gentle as a dove
Because he has a son to love.

Now many and many a year-old boy
Has a father who sees tall Troy
Like a low thing of small worth,
Like a molehill on the earth.

You do not cry, for you are brave,
Your father has a world to save,
A city to build in days to come
Greater than towered Ilium.

SEE YOUR PLACE FROM THE SKY

It's good to see the thing you love
From air and nothing, high above,
To look at where you eat and woo
The way a sharp-eyed god might do.

I have done it under a wing,
Seen my place as one whole thing,
Seen all my farm with the whole sun
Making all its bright parts one.

The field I lived in one whole day
When I was a boy at play
Was only the brocaded cloth
On the brief wing of a moth.

The bays that I had thought so deep
Were azure pastures with small sheep
Of white boats nuzzling at white spume,
Poking their noses into bloom.

All swiftness slowed up to a creep,
Nothing restless, nothing steep,
No hills, no valleys, nothing hid,
Paths opened and showed me all I did.

The road I walked one bitter night
Was no more than a strip of light,
And there was only a gentle tree
Where once vast darkness leaned on me.

There was the place I was begot,
Open as ever a small child's thought;
There was the grove where I met love,
As open as an empty glove.

There were the hills my young son ran
On his way up to be a man,
And they were nothing but two green
Carpets with thin trees in between.

Nothing was hidden, nothing dark,
There was my house, a burning spark,
And I went quiet as a hawk
Floating above all sin and talk.

Ride over your homestead, Everyman!
Ride over it high as ever you can,
See how the sun, the impartial sun,
Makes love and pain and sorrow one.

THE TRAIN RUSHED ON LIKE TIME

The world was growing blue with night,
I watched it from the train,
When down behind the coming woods
There spread a yellow stain.

The train rushed on, the woods went by,
The stain grew tall and bright,
And a farmhouse came along
Burning on the night.

Flames were at each window's square
And lit the snowy ground,
One flame stood up through the roof
And lit the woods around.

I looked for them, and there they were,
The quiet sorrowing ones—
A horse, a cow, a wife, a man,
A daughter, two small sons.

Their backs were to the towering dark,
Their faces to the blaze,
Seven sets of widened eyes,
Steady in their gaze.

They stood together, people, beasts,
That was the one and only
Thing of comfort to be said
About a sight so lonely.

The train rushed on like time itself
On cheerful clicking wheels,
The house went back into the night
That hides all men and heals.

THE SIGN

He was a working man, and he was tired,
He sat before the fire he had lit,
The island, the whole ocean, and the silence
Were leaning in against the light of it.

He was not looking for a sudden fissure
To split the night and show eyes looking through,
He had hands to warm and clothing dampened
By his sweat and by the evening's dew.

But crack the sky did. First he heard it coming,
A whistling like strong winds, and then it came,
It struck the burning oak and splashed the forest
With the sparks and embers of his flame.

There was a cry beyond all human fierceness
In the shattered bowels of his fire,
And the something went back upward screaming,
Dropping burning coals as it went higher.

A blazing brand went off above the tree tops,
Lonely and appalling, giving light
To what might monstrously be pinions,
The crying slendered out along the night.

The man sat on. But he would never after
Be a man who felled and hewed plain trees,
Had common children, and took simple honey
Out of the tenement houses of his bees.

There would be wild things slain and full of honey,
Mysterious stones piled up like a mounting stair,
Wherever he might lay his head in resting,
And bright ones coming down it pair by pair.

His plowing would be like an act of worship,
He would be a man who bends and woos
When he picked the smallest of his apples
Or brought the lambs home bleating in the dews.

THE NEW LAMBS

She knew, of course, that birth and death outdoors
Were suddener and more expected things,
She had watched five blue eggs in a bush
Turn mouths and in three weeks go off on wings,
And seen but a feather left of a bird that sings.

Life in the trees and grass was quicksilver,
Only a moment between the egg and flying,
Only a lovely instant in between
Love-call and the torn and cruel dying;
Man alone had time for sorrowful lying.

But never till that cold night had this wife seen
Life get on its legs so handsome and so fleet.
The ewe was in the pen and nearing her time,
And at the midnight's edge she heard her bleat,
She ran with the lantern light upon her feet.

Yet when she got there, the agony was over,
The ewe had her cud and stood in calm and pride,
And there was a lamb, complete with wool and breathing,
Working for life and milk upon each side,
Their new cloth legs were planted bold and wide.

Their legs were much too large to be quite certain,
But each had four, and each lamb had a mouth,
Each woolen head knew where milk was exactly,
The lambs kept time and slaked primeval drouth,
One north of his late home, one to the south.

The new lambs took their first drink like two artists,
Crinkling their lips as though they always knew,
And both arched tails were shaking like a fever
So hot and sweet the milk was that they drew,
And the woman laughed to see how those tails flew.

I STILL LOOK UP

All I could see, all I could know
Of this man first was from below,
For I was three, and I was small,
And he was fifty-six years tall.

I could not see more than half the sky
Because of this man's arm or thigh,
His shoulder put out half the lights
Of stars when I leaned on it nights.

Whenever I looked up from my fun,
His face was there beside the sun,
And his hair gave off a light,
Being part golden and part white.

I did not mind him on my skies
Because of the blueness of his eyes,
Because of the love behind the blue,
And because the man knew all I knew.

At night, his breath went out and in,
I heard it going under his chin,
And when his heart went knock and knock,
It seemed the finest kind of talk.

I grew up, and he grew down,
But he departed when my crown
Was nearly level with his hair
And the flame that was always there.

I think he knew, I think he guessed
And wanted always to be best
Of all men I would look up to,
And so he went. I think he knew.

I see him still wherever things
Move like life in a sound of wings,
I see him in my own son still.
I still look up. He has his will.

WALLS ARE NOT SO NECESSARY AS LOVE

The father was putting to rights his frost-heaved wall,
His small son did not bother him at all,
Although the four-year-old was everywhere.
The man was careful where he put his pair
Of heavy shoes, for the boy was out and in,
Sometimes the man discovered with a grin
The boy as well as the wall between his thighs.
His young-one was all questions and blue eyes,
The worker had to lift him quite as often
As he did the stones. His eyes would soften
Each time he did and make him a handsome man.
Whenever he scooched, the small boy's legs would span
His right or left leg, and the man would be
Working around the rider on his knee.

He did not think about one-handedness,
Small sons expected fathers to caress
Their bodies, that was what fathers were for.
There would not be so many Springtimes more
That small sons would expect it. Men must do
The things that came in season though they were two
Kinds of work at once. There'd be only stone
To lay up later, when a man would be alone.
Just now a man's lap was a comfortable chair,
And he expected to find his small son there
Along with stones and tools. It was all right,
He could finish his wall by lantern light
Or by what light the moon would give above,
Walls were not so necessary as love.

THUNDER WAS BORN IN THE HEN-YARD

The wild had come up close to the chicken-pens,
Five yards from the handsome heavy hens,
Another mother in feathers, built like a blade,
Brooded her wild eggs, quiet and unafraid.
The mother partridge held her trim head taut,
Pressed her slender loveliness down hot
On her treasures, sat, and gently eyed
The frowzy mothers cackling at her side.

The hens knew this was something strange and rare,
They walked cautious by the brooder there,
Yet they knew also, by some dim folk sense,
She meant well and would give them no offence.
Somehow they knew this slim and soundless thing
Had something in common with them, under her wing,
So they were calm and left the partridge so,
Only they always passed her on tiptoe.

Even the children found her, but she gazed
So quiet on them with her small head raised,
They left her in peace, after they stared and stood,
Lapped round with the glass-like strength of motherhood.
And when the mowing-machine cut down the high
Grass two feet away, she did not fly,
She bravely bore the horror of great sound
With her eyes still meek but very round.

It happened all too quick for hens to see—
Nine downy little thunderbolts went free
One after one, and then were gone for good,
And the mother melted away into the wood.
When the children came, they found not a feather
Where love had held the wild and tame together,
The chicks had slipped away like a dream's slim things
To be wild and wear the thunder in their wings.

OH BOYHOOD, GOODBYE!

High on the sky of evening
The clouds had left their fleece,
The high and slender swallows
Spread out their wings like peace.

The cows came through the hardhacks,
The bayberry, wild roses,
And dew was on their udders,
Wild honey on their noses.

The brown boy stood barefooted,
Said nothing, said goodbye
To more than wings of fire
Stretched up the western sky.

Goodbye to ache and wonder,
To feet cold as the dew,
To burning heart. Oh boyhood,
A long goodbye to you!

The day had wet his axle
Beyond Pacific's shore,
When he wheeled up Atlantic,
He'd find a boy no more.

He'd find his son no longer
Where the cowpaths ran
But find a thing divided,
A poet and a man.

COAST BABIES SIT UP LATE

Coast babies sit up very late at night,
They have an oar in all the family plans,
The father makes allowance for their eyes
As he makes allowance for a man's.

His son may be too young to say a word,
His daughter so new she smiles and nothing more,
But the coast man likes to have a young
Center to work around upon his floor.

He likes to have a pair of bright eyes watch
When he splices rope or mends a trawl,
He gravely asks approval and advice
Of one who does no more than clap and crawl.

He asks the baby how the wind will turn,
And answers for him and agrees he's right,
He gets a dozen things much better done
Having so bright a center to his night.

When the baby's head leans over at last,
The man puts out his huge and gnarled and red
Tender hands and gently, gently takes
The center of the universe to bed.

SUCH KNOWLEDGE GOES DEEP

The dog turns round three times
To make sure he will fit
When he rests. It seems by now
He should be sure of it.

But ten thousand years
Is too short a span
For dogs to learn new tricks, and it
Is much too short for man.

Men who have no sails
Or ships now in their blood
Like to know when tide is ebb
And when it is at flood.

Ones who pulled their roots
From green earth long ago
Will stop in city streets to see
Which way the least winds blow.

I like to know when I
Sleep in a strange bed
Whether I have the Northern Star
Or South Pole at my head.

Such knowledge is not whim,
Fancy, or mere hap,
We earthy children want to fit
In our mother's lap.

REST

The boy went down the meadow towards the evening,
Shadows of haystacks reached across the world,
The night-hawks from the high small clouds of Summer
Fell in a lovely sound of wings and whirled.
The twilight was already at the alders,
The boy slipped off his hot clothes in the dusk,
Slipped off the smell of daisies and red clover,
Stepped dim and slim out of his haytime husk,
He slid into the night and the deep water,
Went into sliding coolness to his eyes,
Turned on his back and let the sweet stream take him
 Past the laced boughs, the deep and silvery skies.

Evening swallows skimmed above his head,
He did not turn upon his watery bed,
The great rest of the twilight lay on him,
Work was behind him, something old and dim.

He rested as he never in his lifetime
Would rest again, he drank the evening in,
He did not think of happiness, he felt it
Cool and curving round his neck and chin,
Tall lilies shook their bells above his passing,
He did not know beauty was leaning there,
He only knew that he was half free water,
Half the light and honied evening air,
He only knew that he was through with haying
For the day and where he had ached to be,
The night-hawks and the cowbells slim and distant
Were the same music and deep peace as he.

SHE WAS THE SPRING

She pretended she was picking green
Boxberry leaves, and she spread out her clean
School dress in a circle round her feet
And sat there filled with earth's mysterious heat.

The other children ran below the new
Leaves and picked wood-violets skyey blue,
Pulled up the flower with the outstretched wings
That flies like a purple bird and all but sings.

She let the others tear and gather up
The flower that bears a white star for its cup,
She hunted for the leaves that last all Winter
And taste as sharp as flame or a spruce splinter.

When the children's voices were a sound
No larger than a raindrop's on the ground,
The sitting girl arose and raised her dress
Upon a bubble of woodland loveliness.

The pink-veined bubble trembled on its stem
As it came from under her skirt's hem,
The ladyslipper with a sudden start
Came out safe in the sunlight like a heart.

She left it floating on its twin-leaved base,
She went home with beauty on her face,
And all the way she felt a wonderful thing:
It was as though she was herself the Spring!

FARMER IN CHURCH

The big old farmer in the place ahead
Fills half the pew up with the restful spread
Of his body. He is a golden man,
Even his hairy ears are the deep tan
Of plowed land, and where his gray hairs are few
On top his head, his golden skin shines through.

His neck is furrowed deep with weather runes,
A map of sixty Aprils and old Junes,
The Januaries have frosted his tough hair.
Somehow he seems, for all his best clothes, bare,
And though he sits here with the shady ones,
His body gives out oldtime Summer suns.

He stands to sing and finds his hands are much
Too used to rough and larger things to touch
A hymn-book, so he crosses them in back.
His nails are scrubbed but bordered with earth's black,
Which will be there when he lies hard and proud
The day he goes back to the earth he plowed.

His hands are twice the size that most men's are,
The joints are twisted up with many a scar
Of corn and cattle and the grain of oak,
With the rock whose muscular heart he broke,
His fingers are the living things he has handled,
Bulls and babies his wide hands have dandled.

He sits down sudden, and the pew boards creak,
He sits as young boys sit in churches, meek.
He does not know, as he rests on his broad
Sinews, he is the glory of the Lord
Of harvests, and what he has done with seed
Is all the heaven men will ever need.

TOTEM

Now every field with pumpkin leaves
Dark with frost is full of thieves
Going in trousers half the way
To the ground. It isn't play.
Each boy with freckles ear to ear
Over his nose has heard a clear
Summons from the dying sun.
It is desperate work, not fun,
He heeds a call too high or low
For men to hear, so he must go
Through the dusk and find the round
Kin of the sun bound to the ground
By vines and sending out dim light
To help the low sun battle night.

When he finds his sphere of flame,
He hugs it to him without shame
And runs to carve it with his knife.
He is working for dear life
Of the sun who freckled him.
He burns to print his own boy face
Upon this curve of yellow space;
He cuts a face that comes from dim
Forgotten ages when men could
Help the sun and rain and good
Powers challenge death and win.
Under his knife a totem grin
Widens in square eyes and mouth.
He puts in fire. Geese may go south,
This fiery grin of small-boy mirth
Will draw the Spring sun back home north.

THE MONUMENT

All the good people of Gull Bay who went
Past Dan Lord's house saw Dan Lord's monument,
He fooled the stars that sent a shiftless son,
He got his monument, a shining one.

Half of his house was white as seagulls' feathers,
Half of his house was gray of all the weathers,
The paint stopped short in a bright swoop of life
Over the door as though cut by a knife.

That was the bold last signature of Dan,
That was the final flourish of the man,
For death came on him quicker than a laugh
And cut eternity and the house in half.

He fell with his white brush and lay in night,
His face was full of sun and his spilled white,
He went in quickly to the Otherwhere
With strength on him and white paint in his hair.

Thereafter people looking up there knew
A man had worked the last breath that he drew
And had a lazy son to be his heir
Who went on living with his house half bare.

IT IS HARDER NOW TO DIE

Where these ancient dead men lie
It seems an easy thing to die.
The death's-head cherubs show their teeth
In marble smiles, but they unsheathe
Wings each side each hollow eye;
They promised these old men the sky,
After sweat and work and pain,
The long ears of eternal grain,
Where never scythe flashed in the sun,
October and April were as one.
Our fathers had it easy going—
Begetting, eating, begetting, mowing.
They knew when they had done well by life;
It was when they had picked a wife,
Begot as many sons as able,
Filled both sides of the harvest table
With men with hands made big by corn
And knees knit tough as apple-thorn,
Each square man on his square seat.
Good fathers watched the good sons eat
Along the table they had hewed,
Eat their own home hearty food—
Pork and buttermilk, hulled corn, eggs.
And the farmers spread their legs
And knew Jehovah smiled to be
Present in such fecundity.

Now we men are not so sure
God visits us in one boy more
And runs about in cloth descended
From our trousers, patched and mended.
We find it harder now to die,
Drop the plow and let it lie.
We find it harder to walk out nights

Under the Milky Way's fog of lights
And feel confident and certain
What lies out beyond that curtain.
Sometimes we think it would be well
To hold a small son's hand and tell
Him of seeds and stars, hereafter,
And go knee-deep in early laughter.
We are not sure we want to rest
Forever, not sure that it is best
For a man to beget all his sons
Here and now. We may want ones
Out past all the stars above.
We do not want to finish love
So exactly and so neat.
Maybe there should be some sweet
Corn that needs to swell and sprout
In fields where all the stars are out.

YOUTHFUL DRAGON

A young snake drinking in the August sun
Was surprised to see me, kindled his eyes,
Made a little red flame of his tongue,
And slid away like lacework, being wise.

I had to fight to keep from crushing out
That fire, those running laces with my heel,
The curves of green and brown amazing life
Finer than any patterns in dead steel.

Whoever is responsible for this
Bitter law of hate come down so far
From dim ages better be ashamed
For my wanting to trample on a star.

Is it because a motion not his own,
But more like music, makes a man feel lame?
There was a time and place I went like this,
Like serpents, fish, and angels, without shame.

Now the youthful dragon who was brother
To me long ago somewhere or other
Rustles the deep grass and knows his beauty
Frightened me from doing my cruel duty.

STOP ONE INSTANT STILL

Stay time, poet! That is your duty,
Stop one instant still in beauty,
Seize the high wheels in their turning,
Hold them still. The blood is burning
To blue ash in the morning-glory,
An hour from now it will be a story
Like Ysolt of the white hands.
Under the wheel the humming-bird stands
Treading air, unwinding song,
If time rolls his wheel along,
That spool of light will be crushed out.
Stop the hunter's handsome shout
Like a bubble in air halfway
To the deer, let the hunted stay
Tall and brave with one hoof up
And the rainbow in the cup
Of his round unshadowed eye.
Do not let the white moth die
On the spider's poisoned fangs,
Keep his wings wide where he hangs
In the web alive. This good
Instant proves the brotherhood
Of all brilliant spiders and flies.
If time moves, the horned deer dies,
The hunter will begin to age.

Snatch this one and beautiful page
From the book of our decay.
Before the bright brook runs away,
Turn sunlit water into stone
Of diamond. So and so alone
Will we, the foredoomed to be blind,
Catch a god young and find him kind.

TERRIBLE AND EXACT GEOMETRICS

How terrible and how exact
Our vital geometrics are!
A cool small grass star of the Spring
Daring to suck life from a star.

Here in the hot grass lies the snake,
Relaxed, with a huge knot in his belly,
A robin warm off pale-green eggs
Returning to an egg-like jelly.

The eyes first, since they were the last
And tenderest miracle to bloom,
Jewels more intricate than suns
Slipping back sightless into the womb.

Then crafty feathers, which are scales
That took thought and imprisoned air,
Superior cousins to the flat
Scales which hold them prisoner there.

Web and nib, they must return
The path of millions of slow years
To make a snake a day. It is
No cause for bitterness or tears.

The splendid traveller without legs
Does not know that he has swallowed
A cousin who turned legs to air
To swallow the airy prey he followed.

And I myself am hard of heart,
Turning the wheat, the flying things
Back aeons on their climb, and I
With never a hope of bearing wings!

HOUSE ON WATER

Behind his house a whole farm leaned
To the sun, and meadows browned and greened,
Whitened with daisies, azured with little
Asters, and green bugs made bright spittle
To live in under the wild-rose buds.
There were common cows and golden studs
Of dandelions they turned to cream.
A slim and a predictable stream
Fell from roots where the white birches
Stood up sharp as New England churches.

Yet never the boy thought out that way,
Nor the people with him. Night and day
Their minds went out the other side.
No one passed there, and the wide
Windows opened on nothing but blue
Like sky in the earth, and one or two
Winged things slid by vaster than birds,
There were no grasses, there were no words
In front of the house, no door at all;
Yet always thoughts went through that wall.

All day the ceilings ran water-runes
From waves below, all night the loons
And lonelier things cried past the panes.
No wonder the boy's years had no grains,
No cows, no crickets in them, ever.
Never for one moment, never
Could he grow carefree, as small boys grow,
In a house that had no front wall, no
Branch of even the wildest tree
Between him and the shoreless sea.

FOX BARK

It was too cold, too quiet for a mouse,
The only living was outside the house,
The old man heard it in a world snowed white:
A fox bark, a faint heartbeat to the night.

A lean and wintry barking, echo-thin,
It went up the hill and down again,
It came from less than half the heat inside
A child that walks by chair-rungs, one-year wide.

Yet that cup of blood, that slender heat
Was all there was outside there to defeat
Those old archangels of unfruiting snow,
Silence, chaos, and the dead moon's glow.

The old man sat up straight, his mind unfroze,
The sound pierced like a needle through his doze;
He recalled his running, young and slim,
And death once drawing back afraid of him.

WATERS ARE KNOWN TO BURN

This sober pine tree never could have known
The maple by him was a tree of light,
A fire-tree, full of the strangest splendor,
Until she burst aflame this Autumn night.
Now the pine stands darker because of this
New tree of fire burning by his side.
So a man long calm may wake and find
By his cool bones a very burning bride.

There is no sure way to grow safe and cold,
A thousand ways the darkening years conspire
Against familiars, against the best of friends,
And turn the evening to a time of fire.
Let no man trust white hairs and quietness,
Waters are known to burn and hard stones flower,
The man who buried his gods long since may see
A strange god by him at the twilight hour.

HANDSOMENESS

People were good to watch, new sons, bright daughters,
Old men with eyes blue as October waters,
But over on the edge of sounds of the fair,
Almost in silence and high pine trees there,
Was handsomeness naked as swimming boys are:
Here was an eye shaped like the morning star
Rolling to stare at me, rounded with wonder,
And speckled tall roosters, topknotted with thunder,
There were cloth creatures with lips quick as deers',
Here warm and meek mountains labelled as steers,
A colt too young to be anything but sad,
Red hens for no reason suddenly glad
And white hens in a panic swelling great
Because one hen choked on a corn she ate.
A mother lay flat, serene and benign,
Ten young-ones at dinner worked on her in line.
Work-horses stamped with planets for feet,
A hundred mouths ran out red tongues to eat;
Under barkers' cries and brass-band's blare,
The sacrament of gentle eating went on there.
Wide-legged calves for fear leaned on each other,
There was a mallard who thought himself the brother
Of the rainbow because of his barred wings.
There were oxen of one mind, harmonious things
With mouths all going one way, side to side.
A pompous bantam stood over his bride
Keeping her safe below his three-inch chest,
There were bland pigs drowned deep in their white rest.
And in one pen a man tiptoe could see
What any man alive would choose to be,
Strength so right it was like a field of flowers,
A calm bull staring over the noisy hours.

NEW DRUM

People lie awake for grief,
People lie awake for sorrow,
But people seldom follow joy
Awake from one day to tomorrow.

But say you are but six years long
And wear the clothes that fork below,
And it is Christmas night, and you
Received a drum two hours ago.

You have it in your arms so tight
That you can smell and taste the varnish
Like peppermint, and life's a thing
Time and handling will not tarnish.

You are ten thousand miles from sleep,
It is dark, and it is quiet,
You have the drumsticks in your fist,
And any minute you may try it.

May start a drumming that will shake
The bed, the house, the stars outside,
And you, until your nightgown's seams
Tauten up and throb with pride.

Time stopped for you two hours ago,
You lie wide-eyed and hear the strum
Of your big heart against the world
Shaped like a red-and-silver drum.

INDIAN APPLES

Indians who sowed these wild apple trees
Are gone with wild pigeons and their buffalo,
Yet still their trees feed stealthy partridges
And keep wild bees in honey when they blow.

Tough as old iron, twisted in bitter grain,
They have learned from briars to run to thorns,
They hide the whippoorwills when they complain,
Under them the shy deer casts his horns.

They knot each twig against the wind like a fist,
Their sour sap bites mouths that bite their fruits,
They want no friend or plowshare to assist
But break the turf themselves with savage roots.

Only the truant cows they let befriend them
And cast frost-sweetened apples in their way,
Knowing the cows will take their seeds and send them
On to the future in small trees next May.

They stayed where Red Men dressed for war in paint
The color of blood and sun faded entire,
Their little blossoms, delicate and faint,
Light up the earth with Spring and sweet young fire.

THIS IS AN ANCIENT POEM

The cock is on the post,
The man is at the plow,
This is an ancient poem,
And it is happening now.

Somewhere under the sun
A woman waves her hand,
With a baby at her breast,
To one who furrows land.

Northern hemisphere
Or southern hemisphere,
Someone is preparing soil
For harvest of the year.

Wars and snows and storms
Cannot cover quite
This opening of the earth beside
The flowers opening white.

The keeper of the house
Lifts her hand up slim,
The keeper of the plow waves back
The wide brown hand on him.

Ten thousand years from now
Men will come upon
This same poem young as ever
At sunset or the dawn.

THE THIN BIRD

How long he had been there he could not say,
Maybe an hour, maybe four generations,
The pine trees had been talking all the time,
Cities might have fallen, even nations.

And now he was no longer by himself,
He knew it without turning round his head,
Something was coming, making not a sound,
He being so still and seeming to be dead.

It came up to the corner of his eye,
He held his breath in, and he heard and heard
His heart going lonely in him, then he saw
How small it was. It was only a bird.

Yet its legs were needles, so thin, so thin,
It was strange so slender things were living,
The bird came cautious, three steps, two, and one,
And then he saw the light its eyes were giving.

Its unlidded eyes were round with fear,
Hate was in them, incredulity, wonder.
Once he had seen such light, unspeakable light,
And it was on the hair of rising thunder.

The light came on, the eyes came on, he must
Shout or move before they were too near,
Something unspeakable, unholy was
Going to happen and fill the universe here.

He must move before it was too late,
The forest was upon him, fanged and swaying,
Those were not feathers, those were brazen scales,
And ages before he sat so at his slaying.

Then one finger stirred, one finger on him,
The blood rushed to his heart. There was a scream,
A whirr of wings. He found that he was safe
Outside the broken bubble of a dream.

TRUST AN ELM TO KNOW THE GOOD

Not by the best room, not by the parlor,
The best elm on the whole farm grows
The parlor is place for courtships, funerals,
Brief happiness, the briefer woes.

The hungry roots can find no food
Under a room with so little life,
Heat only two dark Winter days,
No more pity than would go on a knife.

The tallest elm tree spills its water
Of beautiful branches where the cows
Stand to their knees in straw, in quiet,
Where heifers shine, where little pigs drowse.

Where life goes on whole days, whole nights,
Where life runs scarlet on a pullet's comb,
The elm roots run, for they are wise roots,
And they know where they will feel at home.

So the widest elm bends over the barn
Like a seraph with unsheathing wings,
Trust an elm to know the good for good
And put its feet in enduring things.

APOTHEOSIS

White thunder drummed the west side of the world,
The turkey-cock overheard it. He unfurled
His circle of bronze maleness to the eyes
Of his wives, drew fire from the sky's,
Expanded with low thunder, arched his head
Back on tautened feathers, and the red
Blood ran down like lightning from his bill.
The thunder put the sun out like a hill.
The hens stood rooted dark in fear and wonder
Before this marriage of the upper thunder
With thunder in the lord their bodies knew.
Lightning came on brighter, and it drew
The lower lightning rankling in the cock.
The hens knew something terrible as a hawk
Was over them. They could not stir a feather
Before the powers drawing so together.

The cock uncoiled his nest of swollen springs,
Turned slim as serpents are, spread out his wings
And ran towards the storm cloud's molten center.
Great trees bent wide and let the fierce bird enter.
He sprang upon a stump and swelled with power,
Opened like a darkly petalled flower
To the light of lightning, spread his tail
And gobbled like the high shriek of a gale,
His maleness stood up from him like a sword,
The sky-wide lightning centered on the bird
And stabbed three times with prongs of lambent light.
Where the bird had been were seven slight
Sparks of him going out on the dark sod,
A quiet, and the fragrance of a god.
The she-things saw the pieces, hot and gold,
Of a glory saved from growing old.

OLDEST AIRMAN

Now, all men ride the thin, thin air,
But the oldest airman does not care.

He climbs the unbending stalk of wheat
With his eight intellectual feet.

And when he is at the top of things,
He lowers his head and starts his wings.

He elevates his burnished tail,
Pulls from himself his tender sail.

The sail is much too thin to see,
Moonbeams are coarser napery.

He pulls out light left in his butt
When the diamonds of his eyes were cut.

His last two legs pay out the cloth
Lighter than an aphid's froth.

The light wind takes it, and the spider
Becomes an angel in a glider.

He does no work, he sits with curled
Contented toes and sees the world.

Rudderless, with sanguine mind,
He leaves all family cares behind.

No engines in him cough or churn,
He trusts the sail on his bland stern.

Off he sails with beady eyes
To new pastures and new flies.

His head hangs down full of this thought:
He is going where he ought.

I wish that we on our new wings
Could always be as sure of things!

BOY IN THE APPLES

A boy with wide blue agates for his eyes
In overalls powdered golden at the seat
Stood in red apples underneath a tree
And ate red apples fast as he could eat.

His pockets bulged, his cheeks bulged, and his eyes
Were round as those red globes upon the ground,
He yearned to make his body circular
And everything about his being round.

He ate innocent of any thought,
His mind was centered wholly on sweet juice,
Passion drove him raptly to make sure
No inch of his blue overalls be loose.

It wasn't hunger, he had long since passed
That bound and gone on to a higher joy;
He ate apples fast so there would be
More apples in his overalls than boy!

LAST EAR

One very old New England man,
Who never again will fill his clothes,
All angles, like a scarecrow moving,
Gleans the field ahead of the snows.

He is the last to think of harvest,
All the stout other men are in,
All the good ears, the sound potatoes
Are under the roof, are in the bin.

Yet still he pokes a pallid finger
Among ruined cornstalks dry with frost,
Fearing lest even one misshapen
Ear be overlooked and lost.

The men who have sons in their bodies
Have called it a day, unhitched, and gone;
This man with not a seed in him
Searches for seeds still, searches on.

And now he comes ahead of dark,
One foot in the grave, the other all ice,
With dignity and feeble knees,
Holding the lost ear like a vise.

He brings what robust ones passed by,
His nostrils widen with pride and scorn
At the young men gone in to their wives,
He brings the last ear of the corn.

This would not be the true New England
Without this old man on weak feet
Bringing the final ear of the year's
Corn he will not live to eat.

MOUNTAIN FROM THE TRAIN

The talk went on, outside the air
Was the air blown through a fountain,
The laughing woman could have put
Her hand out on a bright blue mountain.

Along the window of the train
Stood up the unbelievable peak,
Frosted with last evening's snow,
And people could do nothing but speak.

A forest of dark spruces made
A line of lace from north to south,
The woman with the watery rings
Put olives and celery in her mouth.

Below the lace a second sky
Showed the mountain upside down,
Men eyed their watches and complained
That it was seventy miles to town.

Ten thin inches off was blue
Salvation and what God remains,
And people talked the war and made
Noises that fitted with the train's.

A mountain and a lake so clear
They could not have been blown in glass.
Only water and the mountains stay,
People and the wars will pass.

FIELD OF FRINGED GENTIANS

Seven blue flames alone upon a green
Candelabrum lit by cool September—
Only one seven-blossomed gentian stalk
Would have been a wonder to remember
Like sounds of bells against an Autumn night
Or bluebirds in a blowing apple tree,
Half of the world a lighthouse all alone
Upon the dark blue mountain of the sea.

But here in my meadow where grasses were
Friends of mine and all had once been tame,
Overnight five thousand rarer things
Than stars unrolled their spirals of blue flame,
Fewer than deer on furrowed farms, fringed gentians,
Wilder than hawks, secretive, never twice there,
Opened their square cups, turned a whole valley
Blue enough to make the sky seem bare.

Once in the morning of my time I heard
Some bird singing so sweet I covered my ears,
And once when a horned thing sprang in my path,
My dreams for a year were dreams of eyes of deers.
So I looked once and quickly went away,
Wishing the flowers there could not be true;
A man has enough to make his slow heart ache
Without a field bluer than sea is blue.

COAST LAW

Coast women know which women are the best ones
Without the trouble of going inside to see,
They can tell them out in the blue and blowing,
Without a word said, tell them naturally.
They do not even have to see the women to judge them,
They eye their faults and see their virtues shine
Against the bronze dark sea and blazing seagulls,
They know them by their wash hung on the line.

Whitest sheets and untorn pillow-cases
Cry out where good wives live upon the wind,
Strong sunlight and the gale that widens tatters
Announce the houses where the wives have sinned.
A long white washing sets a woman higher
Than one as snowy clean but not so long.
Twelve prophets might put their long beards together
And hit on a shakier law for right and wrong.

THE TOKEN

Frayed strings of twine, gray as old weather,
Now the green of earth is gone,
Hang by the doorstep, knotted together,
Broken ladders Summer climbed on.

She was here once, and these give token
Summer once more will climb this house,
This flint, this hard ice will be broken
By borers gentler than the mouse.

Bright green climbers will come up curving
Plump shoulders through the loam and find
These last-year ladders, and ascending
Curl their fingers round them blind.

And one day when the swallows wheeling
Cry to the sun, Arise! arise!
Summer will be here and unsealing
Her deep blue and star-centered eyes.

These things make Maine apples sharp
As sweet notes running up a harp:
Our Winters close to flowers and fruits,
Marrow of rock below all roots,
Enamel lustre of our skies,
The sorrow in our frostflowers' eyes,
Brevity of our sudden Summers,
Thunder drumming like bass-drummers
Below white Andes in the west.
Our hard soil gives our apples zest,
The spark-eyed chickadees' fast tune,
Wild sadness of the lonely loon,
The salt that blows in from the sea,
The bayberry, the marsh-rosemary,
Needles and knives of fir and pine,
Granite in the Maine State spine,
The wind that's never far away
Around the corner of a day,
The dance of secret polar light,
The quick beams of our sun-at-night.

In this apple in your fingers
The splendor of the Maine year lingers,
This globe arching your hand apart
Is Maine's cool and beautiful heart.

THE WALL OF THE WORLD WAS DOWN

"When I go up this ledge and come out home,
  I do not feel like talking," said my friend.
"It was that way the day I found this place,
  And it will always be so to the end."

We climbed up through this year's bright balsam boughs
  And came out bare on blue eternity,
Tall trees and ledges fell away below
  The long and knife-edged mountain of the sea.

We came out as a boy with young blue eyes
  Might come out on some young and Summer day
And see a whole wall blue with the deep eyes
  Of morning-glories, and have nothing to say.

More than half the circle of the world
  Curved hollow blue from clean north to clear south,
A single golden island climbed that hill
  With a bone of ivory in its mouth.

Silence was best before so vast a thing;
  It was alive, and where its dark weight leant
Against the yellow earth it made a sound,
  Deep and fierce, and shook the continent.

Any man could see that something holy
  Was going on. The slow, blue breakers shocked
With measured vehemence. It seemed as though
  A mysterious cradle was being rocked.

No wonder if a strong man coming home
  To such a place turned boy and acted shy;
The wall of the world was down, and this man heard
  The mother of all life sing her lullaby.

WRATH

Such indignation you never saw!
If looks could kill, these green ones would.
Under the willows at the pool
Sweetness and light are gone for good.

Fourteen bullfrogs glare and sulk
Too angry for their lowest bass,
They blush before their frightened wives
Outraged by their loss of face.

The water's roiled, the rushes bent,
Their favorite seats are splashed with mud.
Oh, it's enough to make a frog
Run green gall instead of blood!

Bullfrogs big as all outdoors,
And what was worse, unhealthy white,
Diving into their nurseries
And throwing the tadpoles into fright!

Giant frogs who did not know
How to swim without a sound
But squealed enormous treble squeals—
The bullfrogs prayed to see them drowned.

But drown they did not. They made waves
Worse than the worst September gales,
And worst of all, they went for them
And caught them, too—the proud frog males!

They had not been eaten, but it might
Have been better if they had,
When would any green wife again
Worship her lord on a lilypad?

A FARMER CAN DOUBLE HIS LIFE

The house a man comes home to in cold nights
Should have a fire in it, by good rights,
A woman, and a light. But men can learn,
When women die, to make the fire burn.

A farmer who brings the wind and frost inside
To the bitter place where fire has died
Manages somehow to take the place of wife
And starts his dead house back to light and life.

He has a little heat to start things going,
Inside himself. Now, out of the wind's blowing,
The warmth deep in the muscles of his hands,
Deep in his bones and mind and heart, expands.

He makes a small world in the empty one,
He leans and joins the licking flames that run
Along the kindling he heaps tenderly,
Small flame calls out small flame in sympathy.

It takes a good long time, but a man can double
His life like this, in silence and his trouble;
A man can conquer clay and tree and stone
And then at night bring a house to life alone.

Yet always he will dread that last defeat
When wind will come in with him, and no heat
His body has or fire will drive away
The final cold and silence come to stay.

BREAD-MAKING

Of course she could not put it into words—
Words on a farm were simple, short, and few—
Yet she knew she had life on her hands
When she had the week's twelve loaves to do.

The mixing of flour, water, salt, and yeast
Was not a process measured by an hour,
It reached from the fruition back to hope,
The distance in between the fruit and flower.

It was an outdoors, sunny, blue-sky thing,
And more went into it than cups could hold,
Like what went in between seeds dropped in earth
And ears filled out with bubbles of live gold.

When the farmer's woman set her bread
On the pantry shelves to let it rise,
There came into her small and quiet room
The thunderheads built up the western skies.

Her loaves rose, thunderheads came up,
Waters under the earth, waters above
Mingled their streams. She put the bread to bake,
The sun came into the stove singing his love.

When she swung the door, she saw creation
Had won once more the battle with the dead,
But these were all the words she had to say so:
"All right, menfolks, come and get your bread!"

A BOY A QUARTER OF FIVE

A brown-eyed boy a quarter of five
Sat in the train, he was alive
Every inch of him there was,
His voice piped on without a pause.

It was his first ride on a train,
Such joy would never be again,
Everything he saw was new,
He grew with every breath he drew.

He knew that everything that would
Come along would be plain good,
He showed it in his eyes' wide span;
The conductor was a perfect man.

So was the man who sat there hunching,
So was the ticket-taker punching.
Lo and behold, the boy was right:
Man after man there came alight.

Man by man thawed out and smiled,
They filled with faith to please the child,
Silence and cold mistrust ran back,
The train ran on on a shining track.

The small boy filled the dusty train,
A dozen men were boys again
Who never expected to be, alive,
Because of a boy a quarter of five.

BRIEF FLOWERING

Days grow, the frosted silver suns
Sail longer through the sky,
The cold grows stronger since it runs
Towards time when it must die.

Icicles weep along the eaves
And into diamonds flower,
The daisy of the hoarfrost grieves
Feeling its dwindling hour.

Soon groundhogs will be up and see
No shadow on the world,
And where snow blossomed white will be
Pale windflowers uncurled.

Such petals the least breath can uproot
Have not long to stay,
They fall and leave their aqueous fruit,
The duskier flowers of May.

HIS HAIR GAVE HIM AWAY

The old man was a wise one, knowing the sea
These eighty years himself and having five
Sea captains in his blood before he was born,
Each sea-father in his son keeping alive.
And people on the coast had come to avow
The old fellow had the gift of looking ahead,
He saw around the corners of dark time,
He knew the men the gale would roll in dead.

A mother brought a child who had no sea
In his inland blood to him one day
To hear his tales. The man looked once at the boy,
Then closed his lips and had nothing to say.
"Tell him about the sea!" The woman smiled.
The captain shook his head, his smile was gone.
"The boy'll know much about the sea some day—
See how the hair on top of his head's laid on!"

The woman wondered what the old fellow meant,
It bothered her a day. But then she smiled,
Some foolish whim a very old man had—
There were no ships ahead for her man-child.
But she remembered this one bitter day
When she herself was older, the day that she
Read, in the brief war note, her ensign son
Had gone to the bottom of the midmost sea.

DEMIGOD

The work was not work, it was play,
For this farm curled down to the bay,
He hoed the turnips with good will,
For all the turnips marched downhill.

At the end of every row
Were mysterious drifts of snow
The wind made of the edge of tide,
It was like laces on a bride.
The boy ran through cool heaps of lace
With garden dirt striped on his face,
Dipped his naked feet in ocean,
Felt the multitudinous motion
Of blunt chubs against his skin.
Amazing life he waded in
And ran to where the horseshoes showed
Their shining foreheads as they rode,
Small one on big fellow's back,
Into the sunlight, wetly black,
Coming always two by two
For love or food, to feed or woo.
The boy flung off his only prison,
Blue overalls, emerged a risen
Little demigod of the sea,
White, hard-edged at chin and knee.
He caught the horseshoes by their sharp
Tails and ran with a strange harp
Full of living strings each side
His curved and arrogant backside.
He raced godlike, and he grinned
Through the flying foam and wind,
Threw the crabs out far each hand,
Snatched newcomers to the land,
And flung them after those before.

He tumbled on the ocean floor
Dancing naked with his mother,
A million times older than the other
Who patched his overalls and told him
Manners, this one did not scold him,
She threw her lace around his thighs,
Laughed blue into his blue eyes,
Laughed, seeing a small Yankee change
Into a sea-thing bright and strange.

And if a farmer over the way
Looked down dully on the bay,
He stopped transfigured at the chance
To see a little demigod dance.

TELL ALL THE FARM

Go tell the bees, but tell the cattle, too,
The little calves being weaned will need to know
Their gruel will be late. They'll lose some growth,
Strangers in the tie-up frighten them so,
Small calves have to eat from friends, to grow.

The dog upon the doorstep knows already,
The cat upon the chair will guess tonight
When she has the cushion to herself.
You might think the dog has second sight,
He sees no days to come will add up right.

It will be hard on the horses, both of them
Depended on the brain that came in two
Thin lines of life to each side of their mouths
And told them everything they were to do.
Now they will have to learn a brain quite new.

But it will be the hardest on the cows,
They will stand with eyes softer than tears
And feel strange hands upon their udders pull
And miss the hands they loved there through the years.
The tie-up will be thick with shadows and fears.

Yes, the bees should know, to keep them working,
But what if it should come as a surprise
To all the rest and they stand with ears widened
And star the barnyard with their frightened eyes?
I dread to hear the small calf when she cries!

THEY GAVE THE FLOWER A NAME THAT LIED

They left the flower that was the loveliest
Unpicked, and gave the flower a name that lied;
They called it *lambkill,* these New Englanders,
They said the lamb that nibbled its leaves died.

The little laurel spread its crinkled cups
Over the pasture ledges, pinker than roses,
So finely fluted they seemed fairywork,
And lambs unharmed nudged them with wooly noses.

It must have been it was too beautiful
For men here to believe it could be good,
So much like love that men must frown on it,
Speak ill of it in public as men should.

For love was something like a nakedness,
Love belonged to secrets and the night,
And here upon the hill love unashamed
Cried with open lips full of the light.

And men with sons to bring up told a lie
And said that death was there with many darts,
They denied their sons and turned away
From tenderness and their own beautiful hearts.

But lambs with little coral hearts for feet
Knew coral flowers could not wish lambs to die;
The white lambs danced to them with legs out stiff
And overflowed with joy on the blue sky.

COAST WEATHER

Coast weather is such live and urgent weather,
It and the men it buffets flow together
Until you cannot tell the rocks from skins,
Where man leaves off and where the wind begins.

This brown bloom on a lobsterman is such
It might come off his cheekbones at a touch,
The way the azure bloom comes off the wax
Bayberries or the green off hackmatacks.

A fisherman upon the sea's high edge
Belongs as junipers along the pasture ledge
Belong with windy skies and beads of dew,
He might be pine boughs, not a man, to you.

These deep-set eyes go well with fog, with spray,
The lights in them match searchlights of the day
Which slant through clouds, through thick and woven wire
Of balsam woods and set the world afire.

Even the houses, like the sailboat's sails,
Are taken into the family of the gales
And have a silver dusting on each shingle,
The low clouds and the low gray houses mingle.

It is good having the winds for friends,
These men who come in from the islands' ends
With white salt on them make my house and me
Proud hosts to the fierce sunlight, frost, and sea.

THE LAST COMMAND

The small white woman in the white house knew
Exactly what it was she had to do.
Seven bronze men told her in low tones,
Living on narrowly in her frail bones,
All there was left of seven who sailed the sea
Told their old last child they wished to be
At rest now and have the aching done,
Be through with winds and passing on a son.
It was hers to give the last command.
She held seven men in her thin withered hand.

The house they built and hollowed with their feet
In their lives this woman had kept neat,
Bright with paint as white as their old sails
Bleached by suns and washed with Winter gales.
It was their house, not hers. It never must
Be taken by slow weather, rot, or dust.
And she herself was theirs. She must make haste
To see no single ancestor fell to waste.
The stars were burning out. She sprinkled her chair,
Her dress, she sprinkled the bright oil everywhere.

They saw the white house last just at the dawn,
Flames were at every pane, the roof was gone,
The house was far beyond all human aid,
They listened to the sound the fire made.
The house, they thought, was built to stand for good,
And now it fell, and only dark smoke stood.
After the ashes cooled, they hunted wary
To see if there was anything to bury,
But all they found in the blackened cellar place
Were old bones crumbled to a neat white lace.

FOUNDATION OF A MAN

He lies in his crib, too young for talking,
New master of being erect and walking,
At the window the west burns deep,
He smiles on the precipice of sleep.

Without a fear in the world of fear,
He gazes up with round eyes clear
Of any doubt the world will stay
The same bright place it was today.

He's had his supper, now he's ready
For night. He gazes on me steady,
Cool, judicious, unimpressed,
Now he is in the arms of rest.

Sure his food will come tomorrow,
Free of words and free of sorrow,
First stone in an unknown span,
Small foundation of a man.

Right and wrong, low or above
Are nothing, he has only love
Around him so and everywhere
He accepts it as the air.

Go to sleep. Your father's a star
Among the first great ones that are
At your window. Love is law:
Your new mind knew it, your bright eyes saw!

SUCH ANCIENTNESS OF HOME

The women of my people are two kinds,
Though they have many manners, many minds:
Those who can endure strange beds all right
And those who have to sleep at home at night.

I think the sleep-away ones come from the sea
Families I have alive in me.
The women of the captains had to bend
And learn to sleep at the wide world's other end.

It took the long and bitter years to break
The habit of going home, it took heartache
Thousands of nights to teach my women to feel
At home high nights above the changing keel.

They learned to bear the unutterable woe.
I have a mother who will gladly go
To earth's end for her children, heart or head,
But when night comes, she wants the same old bed.

She comes of women who never were broken
Of home, the worn chair, the soft-spoken
Usual words said in the familiar room
When the window panes begin to gloom.

Stars must come for them at the same
Window first, the sun's long morning flame
Slant in the right way, or they will not rise
The strong women they were when they closed their eyes.

It is strangely comforting to know
Such ancientness of home enduring so
In such a place as Maine on this our earth,
It shows the shy gods live still on the hearth.

WHO AM I TO SAY NO?

How did the lamb, if there's no law,
Know its mother, first thing it saw?

Who told the new-born calf a blow
Would make untasted milk streams flow?

There must be old eyes watching over
Honied marriage of young clover.

Fire lays the forest low,
Yet always an unseen hand will sow.

Young trees, new flowers, azure fruits
Spring from black ruin of old roots.

Flowers of the smallest size
Are born experienced and wise.

Not a seed falls deep, not one,
But knows the way back to the sun.

If such young things remember so,
Who am I to dare say No?

DEATH IN THE SUN

She had seen death indoors and outdoors, too,
And it was an ugly, creeping, gentle thing—
Always the sad wrong turn. But one fine day
She saw death like an eagle's golden wing.
It was a day of wind, her ocean island
Trembled before the stallions of white waves,
The sun was on the pine trees like a fire,
On all the world there was no place for graves.

And death came in from sea on a white schooner,
Death came abreast of her with sails set high,
She saw the shining sails lean and go over,
She heard the shouts of men about to die.
A dozen warm men rankling with their vigor
Were in the water with their lips apart,
They poured their life out of their wide lips, crying
Of coldness pressing hard upon the heart.

The watcher could not lift a finger to aid them,
She had no boat, the waves ran high as towers,
The open mouths looked like the round dark centers
To the white faces of a dozen flowers,
The gale sang, and the strong men sang above it,
Then voices thinned and went out one by one,
She stood and saw how rhythmical, how sequent
And beautiful this death was in the sun.

MY COAST

My coast is so beautiful
It is sorry to be done,
This breathless island ends, and up
Comes another one.

Slim island after island climbs
Up the curving sea,
Spined with granite, spiked with fir,
Juniper, bayberry.

The balsams march away to sea,
Top to lacy top,
Red squirrels run along the sky
And never have to drop.

The high cliff plunges under lace
To the ocean floor,
But up it springs a mile away
Handsomer than before.

The cedars crowd so close there is
No room to waste on weeds,
Every twig of green is hung
With jade or azure beads.

A rock too narrow for green turf
Blossoms out in white,
A tall house with its door in waves
Bears a star for night.

Every jewelled kingfisher
Has a safe recess,
The shy, blue, lonely herons have
A crystal loneliness.

The ocean and the mountains meet
In colors wild and clear,
There is an island universe
For each day of the year.

BROKEN-OFF SONG

He did not know what had come over the bird,
It lay on the ground, it had forgotten its wings,
Its eyes were feverish with joy, its throat
Was swollen out the way it is when it sings.

The mysterious marks, the feathery suns and moons,
Grown on its wings to keep a mate in awe
And frighten off enemies like lightning-stones,
Lay still, so anyone wishing to see them saw.

Something was the trouble, something bad,
The bird maybe was out of its shining head.
Then the man looked closer, then he saw
The coil of a beauty that chokes off breath, ahead.

It was a flame, which burned yet did not burn,
Terrible letters changing at every turn,
Spelling out words like Arabic, black and green
And azure that blushed into blood with sudden sheen.

And in the center of this coil of letters
A green flame licked, it swayed this way and this,
And two little cold stars blazed each side of the flame,
The man could hear their black and hot centers hiss.

O fire so beautiful it runs between
The ribs, and the red heart yearns and burns to be hit!
O eyes of a god that look death and are kind!
The man saw the snake and trembled with deep love of it.

But some angel younger than the ancient ones
Raised the man's hand, fitted it with the stone,
The worship went out of his wide eyes,
Hate came brimming in, and the stone was thrown.

The fever burned out slow in the bird's globed eyes
And left the bird a weak bunch of feathers, freed.
Yet somehow the man felt he would always feel
He had broken off a song by a sorry deed.

MAGNET

Where wheels have furrowed the dark mire
A steely magnet lies,
A puddle edged with melting snow,
Blued from the bare March skies.

It stretches unseen hands out north,
South and east and west,
It pulls all young and running boys
Towards its cold blue breast.

Not a boy within a mile
With fire on his hair
Or bright sparks in his eyes but is
Drawn willy-nilly there.

Not marbles bright as emeralds,
Not hoops that stand up sweet,
Nor shouts of other boys can save
The boy from sopping feet.

From every house and lane they come,
Of every size and shade,
Where earth has this hole of sky in it
Boys congregate and wade.

Noses will blossom red tonight
And fever dull the eye,
But boys and water will meet and mix
And young feet wade in sky.

FEBRUARY HENS

Snow lies deep. But hens are wise,
They measure the sun with round gilt eyes,
They see it's higher. They commence
To seethe inside with an immense
Growing conviction that it would
Be timely to think of motherhood.
First the tender trial notes,
Then motherhood wells up their throats,
The hymns boil over in hot streams,
The henhouse reels with soprano screams.
The master of the harem blushes
To his eyes, the red blood rushes
Down his chin appendages,
He walks his wing in ecstasies.
Love is all. He scorns the corn,
He shuts both eyes, he blows his horn.
He hardly touches a single toe
Where bright snakes of melted snow
Run between the cuneiforms
Of the hen-tracks. High new storms
Of mother passion mount and rise
Where hens stand in vast surprise
And eye the sudden still-warm eggs
In the straw between their legs.
One cackle sets off a shrill new,
One hysteric raises two.

Winter never can hold white ground
Against these red combs, this hot sound,
Though he has a snow-sack full of tricks,
The earth will soon be snowed with chicks!

THE COWS EXPECTED IT

One stall in his vast barn the farmer kept
Swept clean as his woman kept her kitchen floor,
Never a cow stood there, never a calf
Widened his ears to the opening of a door.

It was always empty but for two
Minutes a day: an early morning one
Before the sun had slid out of the world,
One just before or after set of the sun.

The farmer washed his hands before he milked,
Morning or evening, till his wide hands shone,
Then he went to the barn and knelt on the floor
Which dust was never allowed to settle on.

He put his hands together, bowed his head,
There were no words, there was no need of words,
But veins and muscles in the man stood out,
And his eyes burned bright as a young bird's.

The man was not the meek or praying kind,
His clothes bulged out with maleness, he was strong
And full of lusty thoughts. This was a start
Which he had found would help his work along.

His boys might stare or blush, if they ran in
And found their father on his parted knees,
But the cows were calm, they chewed the cud
And mildly eyed their master quite at ease.

The cows expected this before the grain
Was set beside the stanchion's polished wood,
Their master's quiet kneeling was a part
Of giving down their milk and feeling good.

WARDENS OF THE ROWS

No coast garden ever would get on
Unless a hundred golden little faces
Kept lookout at the ends of all the rows,
Wardens against the weeds and the wild places.

The sunflowers know they must keep something out,
The sunflowers know they must keep something in,
They may not know which green outside is which,
But they know well the green inside is kin.

They serve a notice on the witch-grass roots
Not to run their daggers through young peas,
They wall the winds out of the sprouting corn,
But they let through their friends, love-bearing bees.

Only in the yellow end of the year
Do they grow drowsy and let their big eyes fall,
Only then alertness ebbs from their eyes
When garden plants are tall as they are tall.

BLUE WINDOWS

A bridge of watery fire spans the heavens,
The heat and heaviness of the day are gone,
The thunderstorm has opened secret windows
In the solid greenness of my lawn.

I can look down deeper than the sky is
Along the trees that go the other way,
I can look down to a bluer heaven
And see a lower, lovelier Summer day.

Blue windows in the grass I walked this morning—
O little did my feet know they were there!
I should have walked warily as on crystal,
Had I known I was walking azure air.

Perhaps this is the kind of sudden wonder
The wonder we call death will bring me to
When it will open solid earth before me
And let me fall into an unknown blue.

FEELER OF THE NIGHT

He was old enough a man to do
The final country thing when he was through
His evening. He went out into starry light
Or into the dark, and he felt of the night.

He felt of it with knowing skin and hair,
It was more than feeling flowing air,
A thousand subtler fingers touched each string
Of the harp his body was and made it sing.

His body told of frost before the frost,
His marrow knew the rain before it crossed
The mountains miles away, his muscles knew
The coming wind before the new wind blew.

He surprised the secret giant powers,
Which mould the planet, in their sleepy hours,
He went out keyed-up, alert, and taut
When those massive influences were not.

He looked around the corners of old time,
Mounted over space without a climb,
Moved above the clouds, below the sea,
And found out what the coming day would be.

He knew that he was doing the right thing,
For he was of the old days when a wing
Of wind could break the farmer like a flower
And life and death were separated by a shower.

He had to do this, or he could not sleep,
Night after night he had his watch to keep
On the way the weather signals ran,
On the ancient enemies of man.

THE MUSIC HAD TO BE

A very big whistle came down my road,
And in behind it a small boy strode.

It was morning and all blue sky
And dewdrops afire—and that was why.

So slender beginning to such a force,
So huge a sound, so small a source!

Even the robins in mid-hop
Grew round-eyed and had to stop.

Red squirrels had to cease their laughter—
Wide music, then a boy long after!

I think the music had to be
And took the first thing it could see.

It saw two legs and two good eyes
And leapt on a boy not half its size.

Vigor outside us cannot wait
For the coming of the great.

Maybe only a sparrow is round
When it decides to be a sound.

It has to catch rides as it can,
Even upon one-third of a man!

THE POET DESTROYS TIME

The poet sits breathing lightly, making rhyme,
The poet sits in time, destroying time.
Feeding on stale air wrapped up in hours,
Breathless things rise out of him like flowers
No years can touch, a dozen or a hundred.
The tall and transient thunderstorm had thundered,
But little thought its thunder would endure,
Now here it is a daisy rising pure
With fire for its heart upon the west.
The swallow warms five bullets in her nest
Which long ago bored holes in sparkling Summer,
Fell, and were lost in grass. A scarlet drummer
Keeps a war alive we never knew.
The crowned woodpecker's hollow Spring tattoo
Goes on though the trees it drummed are little
Ashes lighter than the aphid's spittle.
Great men who weighed the world down with wide thighs
Are nothing, but the boys with wide blue eyes
And backs no wider than a melon's rind
Shout in the meadow where they fell behind
The runner that runs on to death and dust.
The poet is befriender of the lust
No longer than an hour of early May,
He makes liars of years and of a day,
He is the friend of young things and the weak,
Hushes a senate, and lets the small lark speak
For hours while fleets sink in the sea,
And steals from time the topaz called a bee.

THE CRICKET

Negro of insects, happy thing
Who uses breathing but to sing,
He loves the hearth and firelight,
Scatters songs like stars of night.

Built like a violin with bows
For his legs, antennae, toes,
Orchestra of nut-shell size,
Half sound, half universal eyes.

Well of bubbles underground,
He sends up bubbles silvery round,
Fills the house, the sky above
With the syllables of love.

He blows his hollow tender flutes
Under grasses, under roots,
Faster, faster, reckless, lost,
As he hears the coming frost.

Small being of the dark complexion
Burnt by the daystar's hot affection,
Friend of the sun and friend of flame,
Wild one willing to love the tame.

Befriend my friends, my house, and me,
Bring in the music of the tree,
Of water running cold and clear,
Minstrel of the northern year!

WINTER IS MY YEAR .

Summer is a brief song in my land,
A wild bird poised a moment on the hand,
As she sings her highest, come the nights
That are the ghosts of days, the northern lights
Burn up above the fir trees, cold and clear,
My country has the Winter for its year.
I know the snow is never far away,
Drops of snow hang where anemones sway,
I find snow where arbutus blossoms shine,
The only green that lasts is fir and pine.
My rocks are the sad ones running cold
North to the Laurentians, the sheepfold
Of white stars by the millions in the Winters,
Small chickadees quick as a diamond's splinters.

Songs of the Summer are most lovely things,
But Winter is a skyful of white wings.
My mornings are the beauty of the ice,
My sunsets are the sunsets that come twice,
The day that follows day is a golden flower,
And men walk through its petals for an hour
With faces that are fire, seraphs meet
And say good-evening in the snow-walled street.
The trees which shine alive against the snow
Are the greenest and the loveliest that grow.
Pity the warm ones, do not pity me!
I have dark hemlocks frosted by the sea,
I have the fight to fight for slender life
And days that come sharp on me as a knife.

THE RAINBOW

As he wrote, the crystal on his window
Paved his words with several kinds of light,
A little rainbow came below his pencil
And took his poem over as its right.

He had intended writing a long poem
With love and people in it, but it turned
Into a small song of the different colors
And followed the rainbow as it pulsed and burned.

This was all that was, and is, and will be:
Night's sky and the deep mind behind night's sky,
Dawn growing green and pale on the horizon,
And then the full flame of day's open eye,
Golden corn and pumpkins, and below them
Red, deep passion fruit and men live by.

From sapphire of the angels down through woman
And so down deep to fire that means man,
From highest, holiest, to the lust and burning,
The universe lay in this two-inch span.

From heaven to the slime and the blind serpents
With hunger in them in the place of soul,
The little reptiles, lashing, blundering, sowing
Stars and laws that build up the vast whole.

This was the poem back of all the poems,
The shape of hidden things behind the seen,
Mysterious lines called God, and all the wisdom
Of brain and brawn and yearning in between.

As he wrote, the rainbow dusked and vanished,
And it was common paper under his fist;
Yet his fingers trembled like the bridegroom's
The night the bridegroom's lips curved out and kissed.

IDENTIFICATION

There is no love so pure as the great
Love of small boys, seven or eight.

They go their long ways shoulder-bound
With each other's arms around.

They walk as if they were bound by oak
Like the oxen in the yoke.

Neither has two hands but must
One hand to the other trust.

Their two heads touching close unite,
The same thought makes their four eyes bright.

When one of them has cut his finger,
The pain inside his friend will linger.

When he himself has stubbed a toe,
The other overwells with woe.

If both of them break into grins,
They smile alike as Siamese twins.

There is no chance in any joy
To say it belongs to either boy.

When one boy takes the homeward track,
The other sees himself in back.

He follows up himself to bed
And feels strange pillows cool his head.

There are no friends under the sun
So one as little boys are one.

NOTHING MOVES ALL OVER SO AS A BOY

There is nothing that moves all over so
As a boy does. Even when he has to go
The way to school, he rolls upon the air,
Swings his head and gives his pants hard wear
In unbelievable and quiet places,
Arches his feet on air and breaks his laces.
He swaggers as a grown man would not dare
Even with swan wings each side of his hair.
It is not a walk, it is a dance,
It is a lilt that goes there, not short pants.
And just so long he dances, then he breaks
Into a run, he runs towards headaches
Of fractions and the Least Common Divisor.
Quicksilver is no so great despiser
Of staying still as a small boy under blue sky.
Wind cannot shift so sudden, butterfly
Go so erratic to sure honey and joy
As a halfway-up or quarter-way-up boy.

HUMMING-BIRD ECONOMY

I have been watching a sackful of talents,
A humming-bird living upon pure balance
Alone in the air, no wings being there
Except as suggestion of shadow.

When he drinks up from a cup,
His bill being down, tail is up;
When he works up at a flower,
His tail goes down loaded with power.
However the bird may incline,
His bill and his tail make one line,
One line that is clean as a whistle
Or the bayonet that blossoms on thistle.

It's amazing to see such a source
Of strength, it's a gyroscope's force
In a body the size of your thumb,
A motion that always is plumb.

From flower to flower so quick
The flight in between is a flick,
He is gone, he has come,
A fierce sudden hum
Is all that there is to his flight.
A pinch of the air's dynamite,
A flying all rests and taut pauses,
A defying of first laws and causes,
A flying stand-still, a quivering quill
Poised to write words on a blossom.
A body that lives on thin air,
A pendulum hung by a hair,
And nobody sees who is swinging.

There's someone arranges such things
As butterflies' flowery wings
Mistaken for blossoms by swallows
Who have the breeze built in the hollows
Of their light bones as they fly
As easy as whippoorwills cry
In the dark trees through the night
Making a sound do for sight
For purpose of warning or wooing.

To watch the humming-bird's tail
Is as lovely as watching a sail
Go up on the wind, or a dandelion thinned
By the wind in its white-headed age.

It is a good thing we can see
Someone's so close economy.

ONE THING WAS NEW

The heart of the house, the kitchen, was as threadbare
As tenements of grass where robins nest,
The chair-seats had been worn to homelike hollows
By different shapes of men heavy with rest;
Everything had been handled by a father,
Passed on to sons and handled as they grew—
Footmarks, thumbmarks, marks of peace and sorrow,
Only one thing in the house was new.

The woman's face had glows of many suppers
Burned in it deep, and she had faded eyes
From looking bright at girls when they were merry,
From looking tender during a small son's cries.
There were half a hundred years of weather,
Blow and shine, around the father's eyes,
The scars of hammers, nails, ropes, and the fishbones
Would never come off his hands of fisherman size.

No wonder these threadbare people held their breath in
As they leaned over the new thing in the room,
A very young man with a wide face on him
Like an apple blossom just burst in bloom;
He was their seventh child, but such a wonder
Had never been in all the world like him.
They bent over the cot, their thin hair touching
Like wing-tips on the burning Cherubim.

DOUBLE BOY

Snow was heavy on the world,
Pines bowed under white,
Children were wading home from school
Along the wall of night.

A man trudged up a break-neck hill
And overtook a queer
Double creature that turned out
Two boys as he came near.

One boy staggered, legs apart,
One rode with knees still wider,
The walker did not look a year
Wider than the rider.

As far's the man could see, the legs
Were hardly half-past eight,
The upper half was a butter-ball
Of live and curving weight.

Their only double parts, their seats,
Were twins for cloth and size,
The upper boy was head and back,
The lower boy just thighs.

The man sang out to him, "It's good
For boys to help each other.
But isn't that an awful load?"
"No, Sir. It's my brother!"

LAW

Creatures are like the things they love or eat:
Bees are the flowers' sweet and amber meat,
Spiders that live upon the painted moths
Become brocades and silver-dusted cloths.

Men who look long on the sea grow eyes
Blue as the sea and open as the skies,
Boys much in the sun will come to wear
Sunlight for the ripples in their hair.

Mackerel-hawks are like what they devour,
Projectiles, lean-machined to bluish power,
They wear the chevrons that the mackerels do
And swim as cleanly through the thinner blue.

There is no other law so strong to trust:
The man who works the earth will work its lust,
He who handles seeds will know his duty
Is passing on his strength to younger beauty.

A man who fathers many boys will go
Like a boy himself to meet the snow,
And only on the grave's edge will lay by
Grace in his legs and the twinkle in his eye.

NOW THE SEA HAD COOLED

Most country people found the snow months prison,
But not the folks on islands in the bay,
It was only when the frost turned ocean solid
That island people could get most away.

The bay ice brought the wives and girls together,
Their world was widened for the days and nights,
They called in person on the weathered houses
They called on in July only by lights.

Now a mother grew as wide in friendship
As her shoes on glassy miles could go,
And a girl could touch a handsome body
Only a handsome sight five months ago.

Lonely boys who ruled their lonely empires
Came on grinning rivals to their claims
And rolled with them in haymows and in snowdrifts
With arching breeches and blue eyes in flames.

Winter was the island time for mating
And giving future families a start,
Bad weather and hard ice brought folks together
Good weather and blue water kept apart.

Men who had been voices in the distance,
Women only clean clothes in a yard
Became one warm continuous substance
Now the sea had cooled and smoothed out hard.

LILIES-OF-THE-VALLEY RUN WILD

Oh tamest, oh sweetest flower as well!
Spray hung with ivory bell on bell,
Lover of doorsteps, woman and child,
Whatever possessed you to run wild?

The woman who planted you by the door
Went in one day and returned no more,
But other women came in her place,
Always someone admired your lace.

Always some child was there to think such
Tiny, sure bells must ring at a touch,
Picked your carillon where it hung,
Looked in each bell, expecting a tongue.

But stay you would not, away you spread
Beyond the abandoned flower-bed,
Out in the grass, with burdock and alder,
With wild things as the meadow grew smaller.

Here you are now, neighbor to ferns,
To wild-rose, not to the doorstone or urns,
And the wild roots cannot overthrow
These drops of Springtime looking like snow.

Did you grow tired of voices and pale
Faces and yearn for wide sky and gale?
Was it because you yearned for the hush
In pinewoods between songs of the thrush?

Well, here you are, far away from men,
Wild with the partridge, done with the wren,
Gone back to foxes and bird-on-the-wing—
Maybe these wild things hear your bells ring.

LITTLE BOYS IN CHURCH

Small boys in the church pews grow
Very fast, the first you know
Ones only halfway up are older
And at their father's cheek or shoulder.

One day they are only bright
Heads that in the high church light
Look as if they were washed in dew,
Their ears and hair are all so new.

This Sunday only heads that dance,
Next Sunday heads and coats and pants,
All the boys have sprung uphill,
Heads are erect, and ears stand still.

One week they are boys, and then
Next week they are slim young men
Standing very still and lean,
Perilously scrubbed and clean.

Enjoy each small boy while you can,
Tomorrow there will be a man
Standing taller than belief,
Little boys in church are brief.

WHY COWS FEED ONE WAY

I wonder if all you can say
Why cows at pasture feed one way.
They always do. Don't trust just me,
Go up to the pasture bars and see.
Every last sleek heifer's daughter
Crops the grass, her mouth a-water,
The same direction as her friends.
There must be some good law that tends
To such matters, for cows at feasts
Are most law-abiding of all beasts.

My theory is that it is smell:
Look at the cows, and you can tell
What way the wind is, without fail.
A well-conducted cow's long tail
Hangs to leeward of each breeze.
A cow smells daisies rather than sees
What is going to be sleek cow,
Not daisies, ten short minutes from now,
And so she eats her dinner twice.
I think my theory cuts most ice.

There is a fairly largish school
Who bar cows from the Golden Rule,
They hold that cows feed that position
Purely out of competition.
They say there is no natural need
To feed one way, it is sheer greed,
Each cow thinks each sees clovers fatter
And has her eye on something better,
And so falls into the sin of sheep.
But I think cows are much too deep.

BELLS OF BLOOD

The bells with living flesh for tongue
Along the hollow woods are swung,
Bells of blood and bubbles of air
Roll in the throats of fox-hounds there.

The running bells of leaping blood
Come down the hills in silver flood.
Thin runners close in on the red
Runner that slants on thin ahead.

Bells of silver and gold and rich
With hunger and hate at fever pitch
Peal faster, vast and round and clearer
As silence and the end draw nearer.

This is the church whose roof is higher,
These are the hymns of sky and fire,
A voice too high for reason tells
God may be talking behind these bells.

And death is no cold or sullen thing,
Death is the hot blood taught to sing,
Never could thing so lovely be wrong
Coming from bronze throats like a song.

IT WAS NEW ENGLAND

It was New England, I was brought up right,
I was sent to bed to save the light,
And so I first began to make my mark
By getting on the good side of the dark.

When aunts had put my lamp out, I would follow
The twinkling wings on every dusky swallow
As he rose over climbing night away
In the deep sky and drank the last of day.

As dark came through the panes, I saw much clearer,
Being so much awake. The stars came nearer,
And suddenly all things I loved and knew
Were bright as grass at sunrise in the dew.

I did not have to turn my wakeful head,
The slender deer were going past my bed,
The boy I loved so much, now fast asleep,
Was on my back and shoulders at one leap.

He and the deer were friends and never slept,
No matter where I was, they came and kept
Watch over me. The boy was not the one
I knew by day who left his things undone.

He was not careless of his hands and hair,
As he and I were when the light was there,
He was clean and shining as a whistle,
He was all spines and blossoms like the thistle.

My father came to see me, being far
Away in town below the evening star,
And he was not my handsome heavy sire
But tall and slender as an evening fire.

He leaned over me, I saw the small
Play and work I had were a high wall
Building up to shut out dead cold space,
My sons were there, they had my father's face.

I looked and saw my saving aunts were not
The bringers of the darkness as I thought
But watched me like sharp seraphs winged with light,
And I was on the right side of the night.

THE CHURCH WAS STILL FULL OF HYMNS

The church was still as full of hymns as ever
Though it was turned into a barn and cows
Had taken the place of two-footed congregations
And the organ made place for the plows.

There was as much good living in the building,
For all that I could see, as when men knelt
And tried to follow prayers of the preacher
And noticed how of soap their big hands smelt.

It was music enough to hear the steady
Rhythm of the cows' mouths bulged with cud
And hens proclaiming they were now new mothers
And burning on their combs with pride and blood.

The roosters were as gallant as a sermon,
The calves star-eyed as any Sunday School,
There was thankfulness at every manger,
And a text for life in every tool.

A man could find a he-ness that would help him
If he looked the bull in his clear eyes,
Any woman had a good example
Where cows were washing calves up mother-wise.

Somehow it all seemed right, the animals meeting
In a meeting-house designed for man,
It was in a smell of cuds and clover,
Come to think, religion once began.

WHAT BOYS ARE

The woman held her breath. For a great seal
Had put his head up high out of the sea
And he was staring at the very small girl,
Amazed so bright a piece of life could be.
The seal looked at the child, she looked at him,
She waved her hand. He turned and swam away
Till his wild dark head was lost among
The wild and craggy islands of the bay.

When the child came up, the woman said,
"I see you met a seal and weren't afraid."
"A seal?" the child said. "No, but a wet boy
Came right up close beside me while I played.
He had his football helmet on. I waved
For him to swim ashore and dig with me.
But you know what boys are. He was too scared,
He turned right round and swam back off to sea."

EPITHALAMION FOR A WESTERN WORLD

Time has not yet grown so gray
That my daughter's wedding day
May see no guests come who are taller
Than mortals are, or brighter and smaller.
Our land is not too far to the west,
Too near the Pole, the snow-owl's nest,
To frighten ones who foot it bare
And golden in the naked air.

It was many years ago
Cupid learned to love the snow
And hand in hand with wooly Pan
Came north to live with the English man.
So maybe, if wars will allow,
Pan and Cupid will come now
Over Atlantic's hills of bronze
To dance upon these western lawns.
For the first round yellow sun
This bride saw was an English one,
This tall girl once on all fours
Crept and looked into the cores
Of British daisies when she started
Life with baby rose-lips parted.
So it would be only fair
For English deities to care
Enough to come and put all right
On Mary-Alice's wedding night.

And if the bridegroom will but nod,
Winged things from green Eire's sod
May fly the ocean, one by one,
To befriend green Eire's son,
Bringing the shamrock, bringing tunes

Made of harpstrings and white moons,
Fetching a small grandmother's wish
For joy like a little silver dish,
And bringing to New England now
The breath of a little Mayo cow.

Come, creatures of Eire and England! Hark!
Come on the wings of westering dark,
Oh, come with rainbows on your backs,
Come with the flowers of the flax,
Pink hedgerose, and the primrose, bold
To open its star to the March cold,
The mistletoe pearls from the gray oak,
Bluebells filling the woods like smoke,
Fritillaries lovely as the snake,
Lent-lilies that make a man's heart ache,
The gold-dust sprinkled on the sky
Over the fields where cowslips lie.
Come, wings of the east! It is Eve of May!
Come over the sea, make holiday
Here with us, so golden, so blue
All will remember it. Bring with you
Little Puck with tanned wide ears,
Titania with laces made of tears.
Do not fear iron demons that creep
With swine-snouts poking through the deep.
Come! make a gentle spot of mirth
Among vast sadnesses of earth!

Yet if the wide wars shut the door,
There are powers on our Maine shore,
Little geniuses of the place,
Who will be glad to come and grace
This holy night and giving of rings.
Come, small natives, on native wings!

First to come will be the slender one
Who came with Pilgrims in the *Mayflower* band
But stayed so long out in the fierce new sun,
Looking for flowers, her English cheeks grew tanned,
And people think she is an Indian now
When they see her go
Under the buds below
The slim moon in an April maple grove,
Bearing bright baskets such as Indians wove,
To gather the mayflower stars beside the snow.

Small Yankees with their cheeks peppered with freckles
Thicker than the thrush's eggs with speckles
Worship this Eve of May, April's last night,
When their hearts pound, when they hang the white
Maybaskets on the doors of little girls
Looking like homemade taffy on their curls.
She will not fail to come, this is her weather,
She and the stars of Spring will sing together.

May Eve will bring the young Maine deities
Under the arrows of the northbound geese:
The white-complexioned girls of white birch trees
To light this house and give this wedding peace;
Paul Bunyan will be here, smelling of spruce,
With his big blue ox;
The woodpecker who knocks
At the Great Spirit's popple door to say
Winter is gone for good, and it is May
And wild ducks going north in chevroned flocks.

Little heifers with star-foreheads will skip over
The bluets with lips smelling of white clover
And pennyroyal, and in from the ocean
A hundred happy porpoises with motion
Like music will come through the azure billows

To this happy night. The popples, willows
Will hang their golden-tasselled lamps to guide
And lighthouses turn bright eyes upon the bride.

There will come the singer of them all,
The Maine white pine, to sing the wedding hymn
And fill this house with beauty wall to wall,
And by her side a doe will stand up slim,
A doe with head up like a slender maple,
And sharp-eyed raccoons
With eyes like little moons
Will stare and point their noses thin and shrewd
At the strange and tempting wedding food,
And round our roof will cry the mating loons.

Oh, there will be flowers and good garlands here:
White violets, hepaticas, the tear
Of an anemone, bird-on-the-wing,
The flower that flies and all but seems to sing,
The ladyslipper and the trillium.
From the Pole the pale slim dancers will come,
The Northern Lights, a million quick and tall,
And peepers' silver songs come through our wall.

So set open the door for these
Guests to our festivities,
Light bayberry candles, break the claws
Of red lobsters. Frighten wars
To the world's far other side
For the sake of this slim bride,
Strew arbutus like the snow
Over the years she has to go.

A KING CALLED

I sat still as still's could be
And let a poem come to me.

A butterfly flew into my room,
His wings were a budding, blossoming bloom
Against my common window panes,
He filled my room with shining grains
Of starlike and of moonlike dust.
He could not understand, he thrust
His elf-horned head against my glass
Towards the Summer and the grass
He lately came from and could see,
But the translucent mockery
Of the pane kept him my caller,
He fluttered, and he shrank up smaller.
I watched a tragedy as old
As Ur or Babylon, a gold
And silver being, trusting deep
That silver and gold would always keep,
Discovered with a narrowed breath
His heart and veins were full of death,
Found mortality and night
In a brain he thought was light,
Eternal light forever there.
I saw my papery caller stare
With eyes cut sharp as a new jewel
Into darkness looming cruel.

I opened the window and set free
The winged small king in tragedy,
Yet I knew he could never fly
Beyond the knowledge he must die.

OLD THEME RESTATED

Rain diamonds on the spider's strings
Melt in the sun. Your hardest things
Last little longer. Beauty, pride
Melt before your breath has died.

Smile your smiles while smile you can,
There will be laughter on a man
For many years to come, but dull
Is the long laughter of the skull.

Pretty love, use lips and eyes!
Look east, the rainbow on the skies,
Whole this moment, will be broken
Before your first small word is spoken.

Rain will build bridges after this,
Yes, and younger girls will kiss,
But not you. This watery arc
Will arch above your endless dark.

Cross on the causeway built of dew,
Poets have always said to you:
Lips are to kiss, feet are to run,
Girls are the fire, not the sun.

HE WAS AFRAID TO GO ALONE

They wondered why the man slowed down his work,
Slowed down his steps to go with a son of seven,
They did not know the small hand in his hand
Was all the hold this man had left on heaven.
A mile away, a day away from the bright
Believing face turned up to his, and this
Hard world of rock and sand fell sheerly off
Into blue nothingness and the abyss.

The man was afraid to go ahead alone,
The road he thought as a boy went on so well,
Somewhere after his marriage, was not there
Any more than the music in a shell.
The music in a shell is in the ear—
Which is another way of saying is not there.
The man was afraid to trust himself alone
With music of empty thoughts. He did not dare.

And one other thing which made him fear
To be without his young son at his side:
What if the boy discovered earlier than he
The people who believed in living lied?
He must protect the child and live the lies,
The beautiful old lies all fathers must,
And who knew, God might spring again
From such a warm thing as a small boy's trust.

I DIPPED MY HANDS IN LIFE

Where my brook ran tame through grass
I dipped my hands in life,
I felt the slender fish like wild
Knife after silver knife.

A thousand smelts from deep down in
The dim immeasurable sea
Were climbing up my shallow pools
To sunlight and to me.

A mighty fire urged these cold
Creatures up warm land
And made them shatter silver sides
Against my grasping hand.

It was the golden sparks of eggs
Burning in them so
They rushed against the flow of fear,
Against the water's flow.

Timorous as infant birds,
With ribs a touch would kill,
They drove like bullets into death
To do the future's will.

They were nothing, being grown,
The eggs within them cried
Like a thousand gods, and they
Filled my hands and died.

I felt of everlasting life
That leaps all bonds and bars,
I had put my two hands deep
In galaxies of stars.

GRIEF

Men are not the only ones to grieve
When they have homes and children they must leave.
The other day, up at the forest fire
On Hunter's place, I saw a town entire
Mourning as if its heart was going to break.
A hundred crows watched black and gray smoke take
The scraggly trees where they had put their young,
Fifty fathers, fifty mothers hung
Above the flames that cracked the marrowbones
Of pine and spruce, they filled the air with groans,
Flapped in wild and ragged consternation,
Joined in a great harmonious lamentation,
Then all came down as one on a dead tree
And stared dumbfounded at the tragedy.
Yet here and there a mother could not rest
But picked up live provision for a nest
No longer there and flew around in vain
And started all the grieving up again.

But grief with crows and women cannot last,
Pretty soon I saw the grief was past,
Two crows flew off, and then another pair,
Looking for a pine top with a flare
Where they could set up housekeeping once more.
This was a greater grief than all before.

MAINE BOY

Sharp-elbowed, clean, and golden-skinned,
Small brother of the northwest wind!

Eyes too blue to be believed,
Too far-focussed to be deceived.

Eyes brimming over, wide apart,
All ears and knees and thumping heart.

Hands like briars on the ledges,
All crinkly smiles and spiny edges.

But in an instant solemn quiet
As a pool with herons by it.

Hair like honey spilled in the sun,
Quick as quicksilver is to run.

Agile as the narrow mink,
Hindside that can almost think.

Big-toe like an extra thumb,
Always centered, always plumb.

Lord of himself even when he stands
On his head and thorny hands.

At home in mud, on boughs, on rock,
The sea roll always in his walk.

Tough as long-cut hackmatack,
Overalls worn bright blue in back.

Into boats, bare feet and paws,
Too quick for snipping lobster claws.

Into junipers without a prickle,
A blue-whet, slender, sunlit sickle.

A boy to make a dull year bright,
Chip of the diamond Maine coast light!

WHITE BIRCHES

In the leafless Autumn night
Birch trees look so very white
It seems a special kind of sin
For the trees not to be in.

Autumn birches have a dry
Look that does not go with sky
Or the storm clouds when it pours,
It seems the trees should be indoors.

Girls with powder on their arms
Ought not stay out nights on farms,
When the wind blows, it will hurt
And splash their silks and kid with dirt.

Here at last there is a break,
Nature for once has made a mistake,
Put things unweathered as a rose
Out in November and the snows.

A POEM IS AN END

A poem is an end, and not a history:
A thousand flaming days run in and meet
In a precious point, thin as a needle's,
And love or hope or agony is complete.
You have it hardened, yours as your rib-bones are,
And it is no more use than is a stone,
If you try using, it will turn upon you,
It will bring blood and cut you to the bone.

A poem is the sunlight after sunset,
The ache for union after bodies are blent;
After the sons have died, it is the tender
And beautiful last will and testament.
Let no man hope to learn from any poem
To act the lover better or grow wise;
The light is not to read by, it is starry
Frozen light in a deer's dead, open eyes.

Yet the passion of a poem is higher
Than any fountain of love's final act,
A bird built out of words always sings better
Than any bird that wings and sings in fact.
White ideas of life are lost in living,
Only death shows how right and bright they be.
A poem is a seashell snowed by sunlight
Far from the dark love-tumult called the sea.

THESE SMALL WORDS

My small black marks
Upon this sheet
With a fierce silence
Must compete.

They must emerge
As a flower must
From unwilling nothingness
Of the dust.

They must force
Nothing to bear,
They must be bullets
Riding air.

Burst from within,
O little seed,
Create yourself
Body and speed.

You have examples,
Frog-spawns are friends
And spawns of stars
At the world's ends.

Ox, antelope,
The hawk, the dove
Will swarm from this
Small seed of love.

Against old time
You run a race,
Shape out of slime
Lips and a face.

Go now, my words,
Brazen and young,
And tell dry death
A man has sung.

AT THE MOON'S ECLIPSE
(August, 1942)

Now over most of living kind
Creeps the stealthy terror,
Sleepy birds and wakeful dogs
Tremble at the moon's error.

The full calm eye of night shuts to
With an evil lid,
Trees that drink in silvery light
Shudder, feeling it hid.

If I did not know the cause,
As trees do, I should do,
Seeing night's eye so dusked with blood
And shutting evilly to.

But I know this is a game
Of shadow and is brief,
A game foretold with exquisite
Exactness past belief.

Now over the much vaster round
Of the earth, moon's mother,
This night is full of creeping dark
Where brother slays his brother.

On the Volga, along the Rhine,
In the Solomons' day,
Steel and fire, whining death
Wipe all light away.

A thousand men who loved sweet light
Plunge into the dark
Where never moon nor sun will come,
Never the faintest spark.

And no one can tell when this shade
Will slide from lands and seas,
We small men tremble with the birds,
Sad watch-dogs, and the trees.

THE FROSTFLOWERS GUESS

Now the blue September is here,
Frostflowers frost the dying year
With stars by families and nations,
By nebulae and constellations.
The slender-footed deer that flock
To windfall apples cannot walk
Without trampling stars on the grass
In each lost meadow where they pass.

Like daisies, white when the year is new,
These flowers copy the sun, in blue;
Out from cores of golden fire
Run the rays of their desire.
These watery blossoms, cool and tame,
Dare imitate a starry flame,
Dare be Apocalyptic eyes,
The great explosions in the skies.

Like us, the small race of the sod
Hazard a guess at the shape of God,
They say he is all eye, is stern
To all life unless it burn.
Who knows but they, not we, are right
About him whose strange name is *Light,*
Who keeps an eye on all that is done
Under the stars or under the sun.

THE LAMP SHOULD BE LIT

His father had the lamp in his wide hands,
He came into the boy's room holding it.
"Here, Son, you take the lamp. It's getting dark
And time this lamp of ours should be lit."
Then he went out. His footfalls went away.
It was odd his father should not know
The lamp he brought was lighted, odd how far
His footfalls in so small a house could go.

Then the panes were golden with the sun,
Birds sang up and down the edges of the world,
He sat up quick in bed, he looked in the glass
And saw how gray his hair was where it curled.
There was no lamp, none forty years ago
That day he woke, that golden other day,
And heard his mother's voice say quietly
His father in the night had gone away.

FLOWER BY THE SNOW

When ice still locks the lakes and trees
Leave only lines before the sun's inspection,
The hard, sweet mayflowers come to lead in Spring
And sweeten the Winter winds with resurrection.

New England mothers are flowers by the snow,
Their tenderness shines through the chill of duty.
Such a mother was this who wore to the grave
Her Puritan and very northern beauty.

Life is never discouraged in our land
Because the half of all our years is bare;
The low sun climbs the naked maple boughs,
And one day the white stars are everywhere.

Between this trouble and this work to do
This mother found the small but the fierce joy;
She was unweary, each new grandchild was
Daughter of hers or her repeated boy.

Flowers spread wider, they have deeper hues
In places that are more in under the sun,
But they cannot so sweeten a year or a life
As this bravely brief and northern one.

SEA WILL REMAIN

In these days of wars and sorrow
You ask me what will be left tomorrow,
I answer you the best I can,
I answer as becomes a man
Whose roots run deep below the sea.
Sea will remain most utterly,
And all that goes with it. The sides
Of earth will bulge out with the tides,
A million silvered fish will stare
At man-tracks sunk laboriously where
They move on effortless fins.
Tall herons will stalk past the sins
Of houses crowding old trees back
And leave a sharp cuneiform track
Of hunger older than Nineveh
Along the margins of a bay.
It seems likely that the waves
Will outlast the latest graves,
Winds will always change their tune,
Fish woo obedient to the moon.
Some hand will sculpture mussel shells
And hang the peal of the blue bells
Among the tendrils of wild vetch.
I am sure spiders will stretch
Their airy tents long years to come
And catch fog beads on the wild plum.
Mating sticklebacks will thrive
Even though men may cease to wive.
And sandpipers on their needle legs
Will hide the duplicate delicate eggs
In the azured high salt grass
After the men and airplanes pass.

THE LIGHTS GO ON

From over the ocean, here in light,
I hear the word from London's night,
Hear the music of Big Ben
Tell England's lights to burn again.

After five years of the gloom
Again the lamps of freedom bloom
As city on city is released
And the great swine wallow east.

The swine that trampled on all men
Are driven slowly home again
To the god they made of straw,
To the blood they made their law.

The old, old nightmares of the cave,
Torturer, informer, sadist, slave,
Fly east before the pointed steel,
And the flames stand up and heal.

Over the ocean comes the sound,
Men under sea, men under ground,
Take your rest now, you have won,
Over your good graves comes the sun!